Original title:
Icebound Solitude

Copyright © 2024 Swan Charm
All rights reserved.

Author: Kaido Väinamäe
ISBN HARDBACK: 978-9916-79-699-3
ISBN PAPERBACK: 978-9916-79-700-6
ISBN EBOOK: 978-9916-79-701-3

Frostbitten Dreams

In the quiet night sky,
Stars flicker like frost,
Wrapped in winter's sigh,
Hope seems deeply lost.

Echoes of whispers roam,
Through the trees they dance,
Carried far from home,
In a dream's icy trance.

Footprints in the snow,
Tell tales of the past,
Where warm memories flow,
But shadows hold steadfast.

As the cold winds wail,
Hearts shiver in fright,
Yet within the pale,
Lie dreams burning bright.

Awake from the chill,
Let the warmth return,
For even frost's thrill,
Can ignite the heart's burn.

Whispering Blizzards

Whispers in the night,
Blizzards softly call,
Veiling all in white,
As shadows start to fall.

Trees bow low with weight,
Snowflakes, delicate gems,
Nature holds its fate,
Under soft, swirling hems.

Footsteps vanish quick,
Lost in the windy sound,
Hushed, they vanish slick,
In madness all around.

Winter's breath, so cold,
Wraps the world in peace,
Stories yet untold,
In the storm's release.

Find warmth in the heart,
Beneath the frost's veil,
From this world we part,
As dreams begin to sail.

Chilling Silence

In the chill of night,
Silence blankets all,
Stars glowing so bright,
As shadows start to fall.

The world holds its breath,
In winter's tight grip,
Waiting for the death,
Of time's fleeting slip.

Footsteps softly tread,
On a canvas of white,
Words remain unsaid,
Lost in the still sight.

A moment to pause,
As frost takes its claim,
Nature's quiet laws,
In a frozen frame.

Embrace the calm heart,
Where echoes reside,
In winter's sweet art,
Let the silence guide.

The Frozen Embrace

Amidst the glittered frost,
Nature's heart beats slow,
In a world, tempest-tossed,
We find warmth in the glow.

Branches bend with grace,
Heavy with the chill,
Yet in their frozen space,
Lies a beauty, still.

Snowflakes, soft and light,
Dance upon the breeze,
Creating magic bright,
In cold's gentle tease.

Winter's arms enfold,
In a crisp retreat,
Stories left untold,
Whisper beneath our feet.

As we tread this path,
Hands entwined, we stand,
Facing winter's wrath,
In love's frozen land.

Whispers of the Frozen Heart

In shadows deep, the coldness lies,
A frozen heart, where silence sighs.
Each breath is sharp, a crystal shard,
Within this peace, the world seems hard.

Snowflakes dance on winter's breath,
Whirling dreams in the clutch of death.
Echoes faint on the midnight breeze,
Whispers of hope among the trees.

Beneath white veils, the stories dwell,
Of love once bright now cast in shell.
Yet in the frost, a flicker glows,
A warmth that only the true heart knows.

The moonlight casts a silver hue,
Over the fields where no one grew.
Yet seeds of yearning find their way,
Through winter's grasp, to greet the day.

So listen close to hidden trails,
Where frozen dreams still tell their tales.
For every heart that suffers pain,
Holds whispered truths that shall remain.

A Hushed Twilight Beyond the Snow

Twilight whispers in shades of blue,
A hush that blankets all it knew.
The stars awaken, soft and slow,
Casting light on a world of snow.

Frosted branches sway and gleam,
Carrying the night's soft dream.
Footsteps crunch on a silent path,
Leading forth to nature's bath.

The air is crisp, a gentle kiss,
A serenade to winter's bliss.
Beneath the stars, the stillness grows,
A moment held when time bestows.

In this embrace, all worries cease,
As nature hums a tune of peace.
Each breath is filled with pure delight,
In whispered tales of the quiet night.

So wander forth where silence reigns,
Embrace the chill where magic gains.
For in this hush, a story waits,
To weave a spell and change our fates.

Celestial Winter Dusk

The sun dips low, a red embrace,
Snowflakes dance in twilight's grace.
Stars awaken, twinkling bright,
Dreams are painted in silver light.

Whispers of chill in the breath of night,
Frosted breath glimmers, pure delight.
Trees stand tall in silent awe,
Nature's beauty, a sacred law.

Shadows lengthen, the moon's soft glow,
Every flake tells tales of snow.
In the quiet, the world does trust,
Celestial wonders, pure and just.

Frigid Echoes of Silence

In the stillness, the cold wind sighs,
Carrying secrets beneath dark skies.
Branches creak, a haunting song,
In this chill, we all belong.

Echoes linger, soft and low,
Silent whispers of frost and glow.
Footsteps crunch on a path so white,
Guided by stars that shine so bright.

Every shadow tells a tale,
Of winter storms and the icy pale.
In the hush, a world reborn,
Frigid echoes, a life adorned.

A Wisp of Frosted Dreams

In the air, a dream takes flight,
Frosted wings in the still of night.
Glistening paths where wishes roam,
Carved in ice, we find our home.

A soft glow from the moon's embrace,
Guides the heart to a tranquil place.
With every breath, memories flow,
In this realm of winter's glow.

Wandering through the frozen haze,
Chasing the dawn of brighter days.
A wisp of magic, softly spun,
In the dusk, our dreams are won.

Haunting Whispers in the Glacial Night

Beneath the stars, a hush does fall,
Echoing secrets, a siren's call.
In the dark, cold winds do weave,
Tales of those who dared believe.

Frosted breath on icy glass,
Moments captured, moments pass.
Whispers linger, soft and slow,
In the night, we let them go.

A chill caress, the night's embrace,
Guiding dreams through endless space.
Haunting echoes, a symphony bright,
Awoken deep in the glacial night.

Alone Amongst Crystal Shadows

In a forest deep and wide,
Crystal shadows softly bide.
Whispers float on icy air,
Echoes of a world laid bare.

Silence wraps like gentle mist,
Every echo, every twist.
Frosted boughs in twilight gleam,
Nature holds a frozen dream.

Footfalls soft on fallen leaves,
Heart that longs and yet believes.
Lonely solace, silence near,
Wrapped in all that one might fear.

Stars above in velvet cloak,
Silent promises they spoke.
Amongst shadows, truth takes flight,
Finding peace within the night.

In this realm of cold's embrace,
Time stands still, no need to chase.
Alone, yet never truly lost,
In crystal dreams, I bear the cost.

The Stillness of a Frozen Heart

Amidst the chill of winter's breath,
A frozen heart contemplates death.
Time stands still, emotions freeze,
Whispers lost in frigid breeze.

Once it beat with fervent fire,
Now it simmers, lacks desire.
Beneath the snow, a longing stirs,
But silence reigns, and nothing blurs.

Each heartbeat echoes, distant, faint,
Life held captive without taint.
Memories like shadows play,
Haunting dreams of yesterday.

A world encased in ice and still,
Yearning for a thaw, a thrill.
Yet in this frost, a seed is sown,
Waiting for warmth to call it home.

In the stillness, hope survives,
Even frozen, love contrives.
For hearts may freeze but not forget,
In winter's grasp, we learn, not fret.

Solitary Paths on Snowy Plains

Paths are drawn in crisp, white snow,
Winding gently, left and low.
Steps of solitude and peace,
In the quiet, worries cease.

Footprints mark a journey lone,
Breath like fog, a whispered tone.
Each step taken, leaves a trace,
In this vast, embracing space.

Sky above, a frozen dome,
Underneath, the heart finds home.
Solitary yet so bright,
Guided by the pale moonlight.

Snowflakes fall like gentle dreams,
Dancing softly in the beams.
In this solitude, I see,
Nature's song is calling me.

Windswaft secrets through the trees,
In the stillness, I find ease.
Solitary paths might roam,
But within, I feel at home.

A World Preserved in Winter's Grasp

Beneath the frost, a still embrace,
Nature holds its breath in grace.
Every flake a story told,
In this world, a beauty bold.

Silvery branches, delicate lace,
Crystals twinkle, brighten space.
Time is lost in winter's hold,
A tapestry of wonder unfolds.

Frozen rivers weave their way,
Through the calm of winter's stay.
Echoes linger, soft and clear,
Every heartbeat, crystal near.

Under snow, a promise lies,
Waiting for a warm reprise.
Winter's grasp, though cold and stark,
Hides within a softly spark.

As seasons change, the world awakes,
Yet in winter, stillness takes.
A sacred pause before the dawn,
A world preserved, a breath drawn.

Treasures in Solitude

In silence, time wraps tight,
Whispers of the stars ignite.
Moments hang like daylight's glow,
Treasures found where few dare go.

Each thought dances, softly sways,
Beneath the moon's watchful gaze.
In solitude, a heart can learn,
To treasure fires that gently burn.

Winds carry tales, old and wise,
Hidden gems beneath the skies.
With every sigh, the soul takes flight,
In moments lost to day and night.

Paths of quiet lead us home,
In stillness, we no longer roam.
Each secret shared with time alone,
Becomes a treasure, fully grown.

In shadows cast by ancient trees,
Life's simple truths, a gentle breeze.
In solitude, we find our song,
In quiet places, we belong.

The Frozen Diary of a Wanderer

Pages blank, the world frozen,
In the stillness, thoughts are chosen.
Footprints left on glistening trails,
Each one tells of winds and gales.

With every step, stories unfold,
In whispers soft, they call, they hold.
The heartbeats echo in crystal air,
Of fleeting moments, sparse and rare.

Chilled winds howl a lonesome tune,
Underneath the watchful moon.
In solitude, the mind takes flight,
A wanderer's path through endless night.

This diary etched in layers deep,
Captured dreams that dare to keep.
Through frozen landscapes, wander wide,
The heart's true home, where it can bide.

A map of hopes in white and blue,
Each frost-kissed page brings something new.
In the forgotten, life does weave,
A tapestry of dreams to believe.

The Breath of Winter's Night

Under stars that softly gleam,
Winter's breath whispers like a dream.
Through the silence, shadows glide,
In the darkness, secrets hide.

Frosted air chills to the bone,
Yet in stillness, peace is shown.
The world sleeps in a blanket white,
Holding dreams 'til morning light.

With every flake that gently falls,
Nature's symphony softly calls.
In winter's grasp, all is serene,
A quiet canvas, pure and clean.

As midnight strikes, the heart takes pause,
Reflecting on nature's gentle laws.
In winter's breath, there's life anew,
A quiet promise, pure and true.

Snow-kissed branches, a silent prayer,
Hope wrapped tightly, fine and rare.
In the breath of winter's night,
The universe shares its light.

Snowbound Memories

In the hush that blankets ground,
Childhood echoes can be found.
Snowflakes swirl in joyful play,
Bringing back those bygone days.

Fires crackle, warmth surrounds,
With laughter ringing, love abounds.
Each snowball fight, each sledding race,
Carved in time, they'll always grace.

Windows fogged with steam and cheer,
Simple moments, ever dear.
In every drift and crafted snow,
Memories bloom, and heartbeats grow.

Footprints lead to castles high,
Underneath the pale blue sky.
In snowbound dreams, the heart recalls,
A world of wonder wrapped in thralls.

Seasons shift, yet still we hold,
Those moments bright and stories told.
For in the snow, we draw near,
The warmth of memories, crystal clear.

A Solitary Snowflake's Journey

A single snowflake drifts alone,
Carried softly by the winds,
Gliding through the winter air,
Searching where its path begins.

It dances down, a crystal light,
Finding warmth in the moon's glow,
Spinning in a quiet flight,
Where the chilly breezes blow.

In silence, it meets the ground,
Landing on the earth's embrace,
Turning fields to blankets white,
In this cold, serene space.

Among the whispers of the night,
It joins a tapestry of dreams,
Woven into frosty sights,
Glow of stars in silver beams.

A transient journey, brief but bright,
In the stillness, time suspends,
A solitary snowflake's flight,
A tale of beauty that transcends.

Winter's Veil of Isolation

Beneath the silent, snowy shroud,
The world lies still, as if in thought,
Wrapped in nature's icy cloud,
In the loneliness that winter brought.

Trees stand bare, their branches stark,
Echoes of laughter fade away,
The sun retreats, the days grow dark,
As shadows lengthen, hearts may sway.

Footprints linger on the ground,
Stories whispered in the frost,
In this quiet, solace found,
Yet warmth of company is lost.

The air is thick with solemn grace,
As flakes gather in drifting mounds,
Yet in this cold, an embrace,
In solitude, a new heart pounds.

Embracing stillness, we reflect,
In the hush, our secrets reside,
Winter's veil brings harsh neglect,
But within, our spirits bide.

Frost-covered Memories

Beneath the frost, old echoes lie,
Like shadows trapped in crystal seams,
Fragments of laughter pass us by,
As we revisit faded dreams.

In the cold, the past feels near,
Whispers of joy intertwine with pain,
Each breath a fleeting mist of fear,
Hoping for sun to break the chain.

Time freezes over pictures bright,
Encasing moments in icy spheres,
While memories dance in pale moonlight,
A gallery of forgotten years.

We walk through paths of white and gray,
Where warmth once filled the air we breathed,
But now, in chill, the heart must stay,
As it fights to remember what it grieved.

In frost-covered dreams, we find our peace,
Though winter wraps us in its snare,
Through every silence, we seek release,
In memories, love lingers there.

Fractured Whispers in Cold Air

In the hush of frigid air,
Faint voices weave through tangled trees,
Fractured whispers seek to share,
Secrets carried on the breeze.

Silence breaks with frozen sighs,
Words unspoken linger, stark,
As frost clings to the fading skies,
Echoes dance in shadows dark.

Hearts once warm now stitch in pain,
Threads of dreams unraveling slow,
Each breath a shimmer, dropping rain,
In the bitter chill, we grow.

Hope flickers in the winter night,
A distant warmth that seems so rare,
Within the dark, there's fragile light,
Fractured whispers fill the air.

Through the cold, we reach for flame,
Holding tight to what we've known,
In the breaking, we find our name,
In fractured whispers, we're not alone.

Solitary Stars in a Frozen Sky

In the night, they flicker bright,
Whispers from the frozen heights.
Shining gems, cold and alone,
Marking paths where dreams are sown.

A tapestry of dark and light,
Guiding travelers with their sight.
Silent wishes drift and flow,
Beneath the chill, they softly glow.

The cosmos breathes a weary sigh,
While we gaze from earth up high.
Each star, a story yet untold,
In their gleam, a heart of gold.

Unfathomable depths of space,
Endless echoes we embrace.
In the frozen sky, we find,
The warmest glow of the mind.

Solitary, yet we are near,
In the stillness, we adhere.
Stars above, they connect,
In their silence, we reflect.

Beneath the Crystal Canopy

Glistening leaves, a fragile sheen,
Nature's beauty, pure and clean.
Underneath the twinkling light,
Whispers dance in the soft night.

Branches bowed with icy grace,
Time stands still in this lost place.
Crystals shimmer, secrets shared,
In this magic, none prepared.

Footsteps crunch on frozen ground,
In the silence, peace is found.
Beneath the sky, so vast and wide,
Here within, we can confide.

Escaping heat of love's warm fight,
In the cold, we find our light.
With every step, we intertwine,
Underneath the stars, divine.

Breath in clouds, a misty sigh,
Echoes of the night drift by.
Beneath the branches, hearts remain,
In this moment, we are whole again.

The Cold's Gentle Caress

A breath of wind, a soft embrace,
In winter's arms, we find our place.
The world is wrapped in silver lace,
Time slows down in this cold space.

Hushed whispers from the falling snow,
A tranquil peace, a tender flow.
Chill awakens dormant dreams,
In the night, nothing's as it seems.

Frosty kisses on cheeks so warm,
In its grasp, we find calm's charm.
Nature sleeps in tranquil rest,
The cold's touch is at its best.

Frozen lakes, reflective and bright,
Mirroring shadows in the light.
Underneath the chilly breath,
We find solace in the depth.

Embrace the cold, let worries go,
In the quiet, let love grow.
With every freeze, a soul renews,
In the cold's gentle caress, we choose.

Shadows of Frost

Across the lawn, the shadows creep,
As the world sinks into sleep.
Frosty tendrils kiss the ground,
In their hold, soft wonders found.

Moonlight spills on crystals fine,
Glimmers dance where dreamers pine.
Whispers caught in the silver night,
Frosty visions, pure delight.

Shapes of winter stretch and sway,
In the glow of soft decay.
Echoes linger, lost in time,
Weaving tales in chilly rhyme.

Beneath the frost, the earth decays,
Yet beauty lingers in the haze.
Shadows flicker, stories told,
In every whisper, warm hearts bold.

Awake to dawn's first light,
Frosty shadows take their flight.
In their wake, like dreams that fade,
Memories etched, never betrayed.

Fragments of Silence Amidst the Snow

Snowflakes fall in graceful flight,
Blanketing the world in white.
Silence wraps around the trees,
Whispers carried by the breeze.

Footsteps crunch, then fade away,
Nature's peace on full display.
Each flake a story yet untold,
Fragments glisten, pure and cold.

In the stillness, time stands still,
Hearts find comfort, dreams to fill.
The world is hushed, a breath so deep,
In this moment, secrets keep.

Light reflects on glistening snow,
Where the quiet memories flow.
A canvas vast, untouched, serene,
Life's soft echo in between.

Solitary Reflections on a Frozen Lake

Beneath the ice, the secrets hide,
Mirrored dreams in silence glide.
The stillness holds a world unknown,
In solitude, the heart has grown.

Ripples fade, the surface clear,
Whispers of the past draw near.
A gaze across the frozen span,
Where echoes meet the vast, cold land.

Time stands still on this glassy sea,
Reflections of who I used to be.
With every breath, the chill ignites,
In shadows deep, the spirit writes.

Underneath, a story sleeps,
A journey lost, a promise keeps.
Each glimmer held in icy bound,
In solitude, true peace is found.

The Frigid Dance of Memories Lost

Chilled winds sway the barren trees,
Dancing echoes in the freeze.
Memories slip like falling snow,
Fleeting whispers, here and go.

Frosty trails of laughter past,
Lingering shadows, fading fast.
Winter's breath, a haunting song,
In this stillness, I belong.

Footsteps trace where love once bloomed,
In the twilight, silence loomed.
Each swirl a tale of joy and pain,
In the frost, we rise again.

Time folds gently, layers deep,
In the cold, the memories seep.
A delicate dance of dark and light,
Where echoes linger through the night.

Where Frosted Stars Whisper

Above, the heavens softly gleam,
Each star a whisper, a distant dream.
Beneath the frost, the world lies bare,
With secrets spun in winter's air.

Silent nights, the cosmos hums,
In the cold, a promise comes.
Glistening skies, a velvet dome,
In these moments, hearts find home.

The moonlight dances on the ground,
While frost-tipped branches sway around.
Where silence wraps the world so tight,
In the stillness, sparks ignite.

Each twinkle tells of tales once bright,
Casting shadows in the night.
Where frozen dreams dare to explore,
The stars will whisper evermore.

Embracing the Coldness Within

In shadows cast by winter's breath,
I find a quiet, stillness large.
The chill wraps tight, a gentle theft,
Embracing all that I discharge.

Beneath the frost, a whisper stirs,
It speaks of fears I dare not show.
In icy clutches, heart concurs,
The warmth of tears may flow, although.

A moment paused, the world turns white,
With every flake, a fractured glow.
I gather close the remnants, tight,
In solitude, my spirit grows.

From frozen soil where dreams decay,
A spark ignites, a flame anew.
In coldness, I have found my way,
The heart, it beats, embracing true.

So here I stand, beneath the sky,
The chill, my friend, both cold and bright.
In every breath, I learn to fly,
Embracing shadows, finding light.

Where Solitude Meets the Snow

Upon this canvas, blank and bright,
The snowfall swirls, a dance of peace.
In solitude, I take my flight,
Where thoughts and dreams can softly cease.

The world lies still, a waking sigh,
Each flake a secret, softly told.
In snowy depths, I learn to fly,
As silence wraps this heart of gold.

The pines wear white like robes of grace,
They bow beneath their heavy shroud.
I drift through time, I find my place,
In snowy crowns, I feel so loud.

The echo of my steps unfolds,
A fleeting mark on winter's skin.
In solitude, my heart grows bold,
Each breath a wisp of where I've been.

I greet the dawn with open arms,
As sunbeams kiss the frozen streams.
In snow and solitude, there charms,
Where silence cradles all my dreams.

The Lament of a Winter's Night

The moon hangs low, a silver sigh,
A blanket woven thick with stars.
In winter's grasp, the shadows pry,
The heart unveils its silent scars.

Beneath the frost, the whispers dwell,
Each breath a sigh, a tale obscured.
In chilling winds, the echoes swell,
A lament soft, yet deeply stirred.

The night extends its icy hand,
It cradles dreams and forgotten fears.
In solitude, to understand,
The warmth that melts away the tears.

A flicker glows from far away,
A reminder of the warmth we seek.
In winter's night, the shadows play,
And through the chill our spirits speak.

Yet in the cold, there's peace enough,
To find the strength in breaks and bends.
The winter's sigh, though harsh and rough,
Holds tender truths that never end.

Serenity in the Frozen Expanse

Beneath the vast, unyielding sky,
The frozen fields stretch far and wide.
In silence reigns, the dreams can fly,
Each breath a breath, I softly bide.

The world transformed in frosty light,
Like crystals dancing on the air.
In frozen calm, all feels so right,
The burdens ease, my heart lays bare.

With every step, the crunch resounds,
A symphony of winter's grace.
In stillness found, serenity grounds,
As nature wraps me in embrace.

The stars emerge, a brilliant spark,
They guide my thoughts through velvet night.
In frozen expanse, I leave my mark,
A tranquil soul, a heart in flight.

So here I stand in beauty's grasp,
With every flake, a moment's gift.
In winter's weave, I learn to clasp,
The serenity in shadows swift.

The Last Flame in the Frost

In the still of winter, flickers light,
A lone ember dances, holding tight.
Whispers of warmth, they softly call,
Against the chill, it dares not fall.

Frozen breath hovers, crisp and clear,
Crackling whispers that only I hear.
In the silent night, no shadow looms,
Just the light that glows amidst the glooms.

Softly it wanes, this fragile glow,
Yet in its warmth, a memory flows.
In every flicker, a story is spun,
Of summer's fire and the warmth of sun.

As dawn breaks gently, shadows fade,
The last flame flickers, the night's parade.
With every breath, hope's thread unwinds,
An echo of fire where love entwines.

Though frost may claim its fleeting heat,
In the heart, a blaze is bittersweet.
For in the cold where silence reigns,
The last flame whispers, love remains.

Still Waters in Snow

A blanket of white lies soft and deep,
Mountains glisten with secrets we keep.
Reflections cast on the glassy ground,
In stillness, the world makes not a sound.

Crisp air envelops, a serene embrace,
Footprints wander, leaving no trace.
Silhouettes dance as shadows do play,
In the hush of the night, dreams drift away.

Nature holds breath, and time stands still,
Whispers of winter's enchanting thrill.
Glades of silence where moments stay,
In still waters where thoughts softly sway.

The moon casts a glow on icy streams,
Painting the night in silvered dreams.
Every ripple sings of love's refrain,
In quietude, we dissolve the pain.

In this world of tranquil disguise,
Hearts find solace, unburdened skies.
So here we linger, lost but found,
In still waters, our hopes abound.

A Heart Encased in Crystal

Beneath the surface, a treasure lies,
A heart encased where silence sighs.
Facets glimmer with memories bright,
Trapped in time, out of reach of light.

Every layer tells a tale untold,
Of warmth once cherished, of love grown cold.
In the prisms, shadows twist and twirl,
Reflecting the chaos of a hidden world.

Cascades of feelings, sharp and clear,
Crystallized moments held so dear.
Yet the weight of glass, though beautiful, binds,
In fragility, a strength unwinds.

As seasons change, and years collide,
The heart within still beams with pride.
For even encased, it yearns to glow,
Through the cracks, the tender light will flow.

In frozen silence, the heart beats on,
A quiet dance before it's gone.
For though encased, it's never lost,
In crystal chambers, love pays the cost.

Solitude's White Blanket

Amidst the pines, a white cloak lies,
Wrapping the earth beneath cloudy skies.
In solitude's arms, I breathe in slow,
Each breath a whisper, gentle and low.

Snowflakes fall with a tender grace,
Embracing the ground, time slows its pace.
A moment to ponder, a time to pray,
In the still of the cold, dreams softly sway.

The world is hushed, wrapped up tight,
As solitude bathes the day in white.
Every flake a secret, each drift a sigh,
In silence, the spirit learns to fly.

Crystalline beauty, soft as the night,
A blanket of peace, a guiding light.
In the depths of winter, I find my place,
Wrapped in the comfort of nature's embrace.

Through the quiet, the heart can mend,
Where solitude walks, there's space to transcend.
In the layers of white, I find my way,
In solitude's beauty, I choose to stay.

Silenced by Snow

The world is draped in white,
Soft whispers fill the air.
Each flake a gentle touch,
A blanket, pure and rare.

Footsteps muffled, lost in time,
As shadows seem to freeze.
Trees wear coats of crystal sheen,
In hush, the heart finds ease.

Night falls with a silken grace,
Moonlight glimmers bright.
Silenced by the falling snow,
A canvas, pure of white.

Dreams drift on winter's breath,
Where silence softly stirs.
Each moment feels eternal,
In the space where magic occurs.

Coccooned in the frosty air,
Time pauses for a while.
In this world of snowbound peace,
The heart learns how to smile.

Overcast Horizons

Gray clouds stretch across the sky,
As sunlight starts to fade.
Whispers of a distant storm,
In shadows, worries laid.

The horizon feels so far,
Yet close enough to see.
Fractured light spills through the gloom,
Hints of what could be.

Trees sway gently in the breeze,
Their branches stretch and bend.
Each gust a fleeting thought,
That unsettles, yet mends.

Promises of rain draw near,
A symphony of sound.
In the dance of nature's charm,
New hopes can be found.

When overcast skies linger long,
A beauty shines within.
For under layers of the gray,
Life begins again.

The Weight of Winter

Shadows stretch across the ground,
As darkness claims the day.
Frost hangs heavy in the air,
In stillness, dreams decay.

Beneath a sky of slate and stone,
The sun finds it hard to glow.
Clouds wrap tightly, veiling all,
In a chill that seems to grow.

Footprints mark the frozen path,
Where echoes softly fade.
Each step a testament to time,
Where memories are laid.

Stillness holds the weight of night,
A blanket thick and deep.
In the quiet of the frost,
Winter wraps us in sleep.

Yet even in this heavy hush,
Hope peeks through the cold.
For winter's weight will surely lift,
As spring comes to unfold.

A Glimpse of the Infinite Chill

A breath of wind, a subtle sigh,
Fleeting moments freeze.
In the dance of twirling flakes,
Time bends with elegant ease.

Stars blink down from endless vaults,
Their light a distant thrill.
In valleys deep and mountains high,
Awaits the infinite chill.

Whispers of the frosty night,
Call forth a tranquil peace.
As shadows merge with blushing dawn,
In silence, troubles cease.

Among the drifts, the heart can roam,
In spaces vast and wide.
A glimpse of something greater here,
Where winter's wonders bide.

Each crystal spark, a story told,
Of journeys undeterred.
In the chill, we find the warmth,
Our spirits thus stirred.

The Lament of a Frozen Day

The sun is trapped in cold embrace,
Its warmth lost in this frigid space.
Echoes of laughter float away,
In shadows cast by a frozen day.

Trees stand bare, their limbs like bones,
The wind whispers haunting tones.
Footsteps crunch on ice's skin,
While hopes of spring seem thin within.

A brook once danced, now frozen tight,
It holds its breath, awaiting light.
Dreams of bloom, a distant call,
In this hush, we feel so small.

Stars flicker down in frosty night,
Painting the world in silver light.
Yet in this stillness, hearts will yearn,
For the fire of spring's return.

The chill has wrapped the earth so tight,
Yet in the dark, a spark ignites.
For even in frost, life finds a way,
In the lament of a frozen day.

Bittersweet Frost

On window panes, the frost does lace,
A delicate, yet cold embrace.
Each flake a story, whispered low,
Of fleeting warmth, of longed-for glow.

Beneath the surface, life does sleep,
Secrets buried, dreams we keep.
The hearth glows bright but shadows creep,
In this bittersweet frost, silence deep.

Hot cocoa swirls in porcelain white,
As we gather close by the firelight.
Yet outside the world is painted grey,
In winter's grasp, I long for play.

Footsteps echo on pathways bare,
Lost moments linger in the air.
Yet with each breath, a warmth ignites,
In the heart's chamber, love recites.

So let the frost its cover lay,
While dreams of spring softly sway.
In bittersweet layers, we find our song,
As winter hums its silent throng.

The Frosted Diary

Pages turned in a winter's chill,
Whispers of stories time cannot kill.
Frosted letters, words so dear,
Ink of memories, crystal clear.

Each line a heartbeat, soft and slow,
Of laughter shared, of tears that flow.
In every crease, a tale ensues,
Of winter's grasp and the warmth we choose.

Outside, the world wears icy hues,
While within, we gather our muse.
The fire crackles, tales unfold,
In the diary of frost, secrets told.

Through snowflakes' dance, our lives are penned,
In this stillness we find a friend.
The past is crisp, the future bright,
In the frosted diary, we take flight.

So let us write under starry skies,
Each moment captured never dies.
In fleeting frost, our hearts align,
Within the pages, love will shine.

Winter's Silent Soliloquy

In the hush of the falling snow,
Winter speaks soft, a gentle flow.
Each flake a note, in quiet grace,
Composing peace in this sacred space.

Beneath the moon's soft, pale embrace,
Shadows dance in a waltzing trace.
The world is wrapped in a silver shawl,
In winter's soliloquy, we hear its call.

Branches sway, the night is still,
Nature pauses, bending to will.
The breath of cold, a crisp refrain,
In silence deep, we feel its strain.

Yet hope lingers in the frozen air,
As dreams of spring begin to dare.
With every chill, our spirits soar,
In winter's embrace, we yearn for more.

So listen close to the whispered tune,
Of winter's heart beneath the moon.
In this silent soliloquy, we stand,
Hand in hand, in this frozen land.

The Stillness in White

In the hush of falling snow,
Whispers of peace gently flow.
Blankets of white, softly spread,
Nature's hush, all else is dead.

Footprints left in silence bare,
Memories caught in winter's snare.
Frosted branches, a sight to see,
Holding secrets, wild and free.

A stillness wrapped in winter's grace,
Timeless beauty in every place.
Breathless moments, pure delight,
In the stillness, souls take flight.

With every snowflake, tales unfold,
Of warmth and love in the cold.
Gaze upon the serene sight,
In the stillness, hearts ignite.

Cold Shadows and Quiet Minds

Cold shadows stretch across the ground,
In quiet moments, peace is found.
Thoughts arise like drifting smoke,
In the silence, we gently poke.

Empty streets, a whispered sigh,
Beneath the vast and starry sky.
Nighttime whispers secrets old,
In the chill, the stories unfold.

Stillness reigns, a soft embrace,
In twilight's cloak, we find our place.
Thoughts wander through the icy air,
In the still of night, we dare.

Frozen breaths, a moment shared,
In quiet minds, emotions bared.
Cold shadows dance, a fleeting waltz,
In hushed tones, we find our faults.

A Lonesome Winter's Tale

Underneath the silver moon,
Winter sings a lonesome tune.
Branches bare against the night,
Echoes of lost warmth take flight.

A lone traveler walks the path,
Frosty air, a chilling wrath.
Every step a tale to tell,
In the cold, memories dwell.

Whispers of warmth in the breeze,
Promises made beneath the trees.
In the still, their laughter fades,
Leaving only frozen glades.

Frosted windows, shadows long,
In each heartbeat, winter's song.
Loneliness draped soft and pale,
In the hush of this winter's tale.

Frigid Reflections

Ice mirrors gleam, a world anew,
Frigid waters hide the view.
Every ripple tells a tale,
Of dreams encased within the haze.

Beneath the frost, life holds its breath,
Time stands still, a dance with death.
Reflections twist in gentle streams,
Haunting echoes of broken dreams.

A heart exposed to winter's chill,
Finding warmth amid the still.
In icy depths, we search for light,
Through frigid reflections, we take flight.

Shadows flicker, dance and play,
Frigid nights blend into day.
Reflections fade with dawn's first glow,
Yet in our hearts, the cold winds blow.

The Resounding Quiet of a Snow-Blanketed World

In the hush of falling snow,
Whispers linger, soft and slow.
Crisp air dances, faint and bright,
Silence cradles the fading light.

Footsteps muffled, all is still,
Nature's canvas, white with chill.
Trees stand tall in frosty grace,
Time suspended in this place.

Every flake a unique song,
Wrapped in blankets, silent throng.
Night descends, a velvet shroud,
Under stars, the world is bowed.

Frozen moments, breath on glass,
Memories caught, as shadows pass.
Cold embraces, tender touch,
In this stillness, we feel so much.

A Heart Adrift in Wintry Stillness

Beneath the weight of winter's breath,
A heart wanders, lost in depths.
Snowflakes twirl like fragile dreams,
Drifting softly, or so it seems.

In solitude, the winds do weep,
Calling softly, luring deep.
I wander through the frozen hush,
In this stillness, hear the rush.

Stars awaken in the midnight sky,
The heart yearns, a muted sigh.
Cold shadows dance upon the snow,
Yearning for warmth, the heart's glow.

Yet in the quiet, peace is found,
In frost-kissed air, love surrounds.
A whispered promise in the chill,
In winter's grasp, the heart is still.

Frost-kissed Reminders of Days Long Past

Memories hidden in the snow,
Frost-kissed whispers, soft and low.
Echoes of laughter, warm and bright,
Now are shadows in fading light.

Each flake a story, glimmering white,
Reminders of days wrapped in light.
Frozen moments, held in time,
A bittersweet, nostalgic rhyme.

Footprints linger, then they fade,
In the silence, dreams are laid.
Winter's breath, a chilling sigh,
But in that frost, our hearts will fly.

Brought together, yet apart,
Frost-kissed echoes stir the heart.
Through the still, the past remains,
In every flake, love still reigns.

The Lonely Journey of a Snowdrift

A snowdrift rises, tall and wide,
In winter's grasp, it cannot hide.
Settled softly on the ground,
Whispers of journeys all around.

It bends beneath the weight of time,
A solitary, silent climb.
Frosty edges, worn and cold,
Echo tales that must be told.

The wind howls, a distant call,
Yet the snowdrift stands so tall.
Layer by layer, history made,
In every drift, memories laid.

Beneath the moon, it softly glows,
A quiet sentinel, winter's prose.
Endless dreams in cotton white,
A lonely journey, still in flight.

Crystal Shards of Isolation

In the quiet of the night,
Shimmers catch the pale light,
Fragments of a distant dream,
Soft whispers, silent scream.

Frozen silence wraps the air,
Loneliness is everywhere,
Each glimmer tells a story,
Of fading hope and past glory.

Wandering through this frozen land,
Tracing lines with trembling hand,
Crystal shards my only kin,
Reflecting where I have been.

Fractured visions fill my sight,
Ghostly forms in silver white,
Isolated, yet I roam,
Searching still for my lost home.

In the depths of winter's cast,
Each moment feels like the last,
Yet within each icy shard,
Lies the beauty, though it's hard.

Solitary Glaciers

Beneath the wide, unyielding sky,
Lies a glacier, slow to cry,
Its ancient eyes gaze far and wide,
Frozen tales it cannot hide.

Cracks and crevices reveal
Secrets only time can seal,
With each thaw the stories pour,
Of loneliness and ancient lore.

Waves of ice in somber hues,
Silently absorbing blues,
Guarding whispers of the past,
Solitary, standing fast.

Each passing storm, a solemn vow,
Nature's grip will not allow,
The glacier shifts, yet stays the same,
Loneliness is its only claim.

Among the mountains, proud and tall,
Glaciers stand, serene, enthralled,
In their silence, wisdom sings,
Of solitude that winter brings.

Echoes Through the Frost

In the stillness of the night,
Echoes dance in silver light,
Footfalls lost in frosted air,
Whispers drifting, light as prayer.

Each sound mulled in icy breath,
Reminders of the warmth of death,
Loneliness calls through the white,
Carried softly, out of sight.

Shadows cast by ancient trees,
Telling tales upon the breeze,
Through the frost, the echoes play,
Of hearts once bold, now turned to clay.

In this realm of frozen peace,
Hope and sorrow find release,
As I listen to the night,
Echoes filling space with light.

Through the chill, the whispers grow,
Tales of yore, a gentle flow,
In the frost, they intertwine,
Reminding me of love's design.

The Winter's Heart

Deep within the frozen land,
Beats a heart both cold and grand,
Wrapped in layers, soft and stark,
The winter's pulse ignites the dark.

Every flake that falls to rest,
Whispers gently, nature's quest,
Painting white on earth's embrace,
As silence finds a warming space.

Icicles hang like frozen tears,
Marking out the passing years,
In their shimmer, stories flow,
Of love that's lost and pain that grows.

Yet within the chill, a flame,
Rests beneath the brittle name,
Winter's heart, so fierce, so bright,
Holds the promise of delight.

Through the frost, may hope be seen,
In the stark and shadowed sheen,
For the winter's heart beats true,
And always finds the strength anew.

Frost and Solitude

In the stillness of the night,
Frost blankets the world tight.
Stars glimmer in cold air,
Echoes of a dreamer's prayer.

Trees stand rigid, bare and bright,
Whispers carried by moonlight.
Footsteps crunch on crystal ground,
Silence is the only sound.

Shadows dance with shadows near,
In this realm, all is clear.
A heart finds peace in frost's embrace,
In solitude, we find our space.

Breath is visible, a ghostly wisp,
Loneliness lingers with every gasp.
But beauty lies in winter's cold,
A story of warmth waiting to be told.

The stars seem to sway with ease,
Guided by the whispering breeze.
Frost and solitude, a gentle hand,
In this frozen, enchanted land.

Whispers Beneath the Ice

Beneath the ice, secrets sleep,
Silent promises they keep.
Whispers soft, like snowflakes fall,
Each one answering winter's call.

A world transformed in frosted hue,
Time stands still, as if anew.
Memories drift in chilly air,
Carried through the maiden's prayer.

Ripples twist beneath the freeze,
Nature's heart beats, pulses wheeze.
What was lost now finds its way,
In the quiet of the day.

Echoes of joy and sorrow blend,
In the frost, they seem to mend.
Life's stories written in the snow,
Whispers beneath, the softest flow.

With each step, the ground will sigh,
A gentle touch, the reasons why.
Through the still, a voice aligns,
In whispers, nature's truth defines.

A Secluded Frostscape

Amidst the trees, a frosty view,
Where winter's breath paints all anew.
A secret path, so soft and white,
Leads to a world of pure delight.

Brittle branches softly sway,
As shadows dance at end of day.
Crisp air fills the lungs with glee,
In this serene, enchanted spree.

Each step whispers tales unsaid,
In this frostscape, joys are bred.
Nature cloaked in silvery sheen,
A moment's peace, the rarest scene.

The horizon glows with soft embrace,
As twilight casts its gentle grace.
In solitude where hearts convene,
A secluded frostscape, pure and clean.

Beneath the stars, a quiet night,
In winter's arms, all feels right.
Here, life slows its frantic pace,
In the quietude, we find our place.

Melancholy in White

The world adorned in pale attire,
A canvas painted by winter's fire.
Melancholy hangs in the air,
An echo of a softened stare.

Snowflakes weep on frozen ground,
A silent song, without a sound.
Wisps of clouds like lost forlorn,
In winter's grip, a heart feels worn.

Beneath the sky, a somber light,
Captures dreams in ghostly flight.
In every drift, a tale is spun,
Of laughter lost and joys outrun.

But in the stillness, hope survives,
For spring will come, and so it thrives.
Until that day, in quiet fight,
We find our peace in melancholy white.

Through frosted panes, the world retreats,
And as the heart with slow beat meets,
The winter's chill, a cloak, a shield,
In this white haven, pain is healed.

So let us wander hand in hand,
In this vast, enchanted land.
For in the melancholy's embrace,
We'll find our warmth, our sacred space.

Lonesome Echoes in Frost

In the quiet of a winter's night,
Footsteps fade, lost from sight.
Whispers slide through the air,
A soft reminder of despair.

Moonlight glistens on the trees,
Carving shadows with a freeze.
Each sigh hangs in silence still,
Haunting echoes, hearts to fill.

Branches creak, a gentle moan,
Nature's voice, a lonesome tone.
Snowflakes dance without a trace,
Fleeting warmth in a cold embrace.

Embers flicker, warmth declines,
Memories wrapped in icy vines.
Time drifts slowly, bitter cold,
Stories shared, but never told.

The night stretches, vast and wide,
Carrying dreams where shadows bide.
Lonesome echoes call my name,
In the frost, who feels the same?

The Frostbitten Silence

Beneath the weight of winter's breath,
Lies the silent call of death.
Every corner wrapped in white,
The world sleeps in cold twilight.

Frozen branches stand so tall,
Guarding secrets, cloaked in pall.
No birds sing, no rivers flow,
Just the hush of falling snow.

Footsteps lead to hollow dreams,
Silence breaks with frozen beams.
In this stillness, time stands still,
Calmness depths my heart to fill.

Stars above, a distant light,
Pierce the veil of endless night.
Frostbitten, my soul entwined,
In this silence, peace I find.

Every breath a crystal shard,
Held in tension, ever hard.
The frost clings to memory's trace,
In this still, eternal space.

A World Locked in Chill

Under layers of drifting snow,
A world sleeps without a glow.
The air is crisp, the night is deep,
In frozen dreams, the shadows creep.

Fields of white, an endless sea,
Nature's art, wild and free.
Each flake unique, a fleeting grace,
In this chill, I find my place.

Icicles hang from rooftops high,
Catching whispers of the sky.
Time moves slow, the clock unwinds,
In these moments, peace I find.

With every breath, a mist of air,
Embracing cold, the heart laid bare.
Wrapped in silence, softly still,
This world lost in winter's thrill.

Here the stars twinkle, frost-kissed bright,
Guiding dreams through the night.
Together we dance, the sky we fill,
In a world forever locked in chill.

The Subzero Solace

In a realm of glistening frost,
Where warmth is weary, hope embossed.
Subzero winds cradle my thoughts,
In their embrace, all fear is caught.

Lonely roads stretch far and wide,
Veiling secrets that abide.
Wrapped in blankets made of snow,
Here in comfort, silence grows.

Stars above, like whispered tales,
Dance in shadows, softly sail.
The night is young, yet full of grace,
In the solace of this space.

Each shivering branch tells a story,
Of fading light and lost glory.
Here I stand, my spirit flies,
Beneath a moonlit winter sky.

This stillness brings a bittersweet,
A tender moment, slow and fleet.
In subzero climes, I find release,
A fragile heart, wrapped in peace.

Shattered Glass and Loneliness

In a room full of echoes, cold and bare,
A mirror reflects the weight of despair.
Fragments of dreams lie scattered around,
Whispers of memories, lost and unfound.

Silent shadows dance on the wall,
Each piece holds a story, a rise, and a fall.
Loneliness lingers in every crack,
Time slips away, but will not turn back.

The light filters through in jagged lines,
Casting dark patterns where doubt entwines.
I reach for the pieces, hoping to heal,
But the heart's fragile glass is hard to conceal.

Outside the window, life plays its part,
Yet in here, I'm trapped with a heavy heart.
Shattered reflections, memories they tease,
Loneliness echoes, a haunting breeze.

So I gather the shards, make something new,
Out of the chaos, a clearer view.
Though pain leaves a mark, and scars may remain,
Out of shattered glass, strength can be gained.

Hushed by the Snow

A blanket of white covers the ground,
Silence wraps the world, peace is profound.
Footprints are hidden, all traces erased,
Under the snow, life fits in a haste.

The trees wear garments of glistening frost,
In this hush of winter, I ponder the cost.
Where are the colors, the laughter, the sound?
As the world pauses, we gather around.

Breathe in the chill of the crisp, cold air,
Each breath a promise, a chance to repair.
Nature holds secrets in shadows and light,
In the depths of winter, our hearts feel the night.

But beauty blooms softly, beneath sparkling white,
Hope dances lightly through the stillness of night.
Hushed by the snow, we find solace, we dream,
In this tranquil moment, life's more than it seems.

As winter whispers, groans, and sighs,
We learn to listen through softening skies.
Harmony rests in the cozy embrace,
Hushed by the snow, we discover our place.

Desolate Landscapes

Vast fields stretch barren, a lonely expanse,
Echoes of silence in nature's own dance.
Mountains stand stoic against the gray sky,
Whispers of history in every sigh.

The winds carry tales of times long gone,
Over the valleys, they drift and they yawn.
Cacti and shadows mark a rugged terrain,
Beauty and hardship intertwined with the pain.

Colors of dusk paint the edges of day,
In desolate landscapes, lost dreams lay.
Sunsets are vivid, but nights can be cold,
In the heart of the wild, the forgotten unfold.

Yet amidst the harshness, resilience blooms bright,
Life dares to flourish in the absence of light.
From cracks in the earth, tiny flowers emerge,
In desolate places, a quiet urge.

So I walk through the barren, my spirits held high,
Finding beauty in places that most pass by.
Desolate landscapes teach lessons profound,
In the stillness of nature, connection is found.

Solitude Beneath Snowflakes

Snowflakes drift gently, soft whispers of time,
Each one a moment, a solitary rhyme.
They blanket the earth in a shroud of white,
Brushing away footsteps, dimming the light.

In the quiet of winter, I breathe in the air,
Solitude nestles within frosty care.
A world made of stillness, a canvas so pure,
In this tranquil shelter, I find my allure.

Each flake tells a story, unique in its fall,
Gathering softly, they answer the call.
Under the snow, there lies dormant hope,
In the heart of the winter, we learn how to cope.

Outside the window, the world may seem bare,
But deep in the silence, I feel your stare.
Solitude beckons, with arms open wide,
In this snow-covered realm, no need to hide.

As the evening falls, the stars start to glow,
In solitude's embrace, I finally know.
Beneath the soft snowflakes, my spirit takes flight,
In the stillness of winter, I find my light.

Glistening Loneliness

In the quiet night, stars gleam,
Silent whispers, a forgotten dream.
A single tear on frozen ground,
Lonely heartbeats, no solace found.

Shadows dance in silver light,
Echoes linger, taking flight.
Footsteps fade in the chilling air,
Lost in thoughts, adrift, a snare.

Frosted windows, a love once near,
Now just shadows, whispers unclear.
A fragile heart cloaked in fear,
Seeking warmth, but it disappears.

Through the mist, the memories creep,
In silence deep, secrets keep.
Glistening tears, a soft refrain,
In the stillness, only the pain.

Yet in the dark, hope glimmers bright,
A flicker of love amidst the night.
For in sorrow, strength can bloom,
A heart's resilience breaks the gloom.

Crystalline Thoughts

In the stillness, ideas collide,
Thoughts like crystals cannot hide.
Shimmering facets of dreams untold,
Reflections of visions, pure and bold.

Each fragment sparkles in the mind,
A tapestry of what we find.
Spirals of wonder taking flight,
Illuminating the depths of night.

Beneath the surface, layers grow,
Tales of joy, of sorrow's flow.
In every crystal, a story lies,
Glimmers of truth beneath the skies.

Pouring thoughts like morning dew,
Clarity in every view.
With every angle, new designs,
In crystalline paths, wisdom finds.

Let the brilliance guide your way,
Through stormy nights and brightening day.
Illumine the darkness with vibrant dreams,
For thoughts like crystals burst at the seams.

Shroud of the North Wind

A blanket white, the world adorned,
The North Wind's breath, a tale reborn.
Whispers carry through pine and snow,
In every flake, the chill does flow.

Silhouettes of trees in twilight fade,
While gentle storms weave a cold cascade.
Branches bow beneath the weight,
Nature's sigh, a whispered fate.

Frosty fingers trace the ground,
In every corner, secrets found.
Echoes linger, haunting, clear,
In the stillness, we draw near.

Through the darkness, the moonlight gleams,
A guiding star for all our dreams.
Wrapped in silver, the night a shroud,
In the distance, whispers loud.

Yet with dawn, the chill will wane,
Leaving warmth in its gentle reign.
From the North Wind's breath, life will spring,
A tapestry of hues, birthed from spring.

Celestial Ice

Above the world, the heavens gleam,
In frozen realms, where starlights beam.
Celestial ice, a mystical dance,
Capturing dreams in a starlit trance.

Fragments of comets trail behind,
Whispers of wishes, intertwined.
In the vastness, silence reigns,
A symphony of hopes, love's refrains.

Galaxies twirl in the night's embrace,
In the depths of dark, we find our place.
Crystalline wonders, paths we trace,
In the shimmering void, a gentle grace.

Each frozen moment, a story spun,
Echoes of laughter, forgotten fun.
As time drifts softly, it holds us tight,
In celestial ice, a comforting light.

Through the cosmos, our spirits soar,
Beyond the stars, forevermore.
In the embrace of the endless skies,
Celestial ice, where wonder lies.

Desolate Glade

A shadowed path winds deep and low,
Leaves whisper tales of long ago.
Moss blankets stones, so soft and green,
In this quiet place, all feels unseen.

A chill caress upon the air,
Time stands still, lost in despair.
Branches reach like fingers cold,
Guard secrets of lives not told.

The echo of footsteps fades away,
As twilight beckons the end of day.
Light dances dimly where shadows creep,
In the desolate glade, silence sleeps.

A breeze stirs softly, a gentle sigh,
Nature's breath beneath the sky.
Yet solace waits in the stillness found,
In the embrace of the earth, profound.

With every rustle and haunting call,
A reminder of life beyond the fall.
The desolate glade, a sacred space,
Holds the essence of a forgotten place.

Echoes in Crystal Silence

In the heart of winter, silence reigns,
A landscape veiled in icy chains.
The world transformed, so pure, so bright,
Under the spell of the starry night.

Each flake that falls, a whispered dream,
Dancing down, a silken beam.
Frozen thoughts in the frosty air,
Echoes linger everywhere.

With every breath, the stillness swells,
A symphony that nature tells.
In crystal halls where shadows play,
The echoes roam, then drift away.

Branches crowned in silver lace,
Reflect the moon's soft, tender grace.
In this calm, the heart finds peace,
In winter's hold, the world's release.

As night descends and silence grows,
A tranquil beauty softly flows.
In echoes, deep within the night,
Crystal silence speaks of pure delight.

Serenity in the Chill

A frosty dawn breaks with a sigh,
Painting the world with a tender eye.
In the crisp air, a stillness unfolds,
Whispers of warmth in twilight's holds.

Snow blankets the ground, soft and white,
Embracing all in sheer delight.
Each breath releases a clouded dream,
In the solitude where reflections gleam.

A solitary figure walks alone,
Amidst the beauty, the chill is known.
Yet peace has wrapped this quiet space,
In gentle whispers, the soul finds grace.

Time seems to pause as moments blend,
In the chill of serenity, a friend.
The heart beats slow, in rhythm with earth,
Embracing the quiet, a sense of rebirth.

As twilight falls with colors soft,
The world sighs deeply, drifting aloft.
In the chill of night, the spirit flies,
Finding serenity beneath the skies.

A Frost-kissed Reverie

Beneath a canopy of twilight's hue,
Lies a frosted dream, both old and new.
Each breath a mist, a gentle sigh,
In this reverie where moments lie.

The world adorned in a shimmering gown,
In fragile beauty, the ice settles down.
Whispers carried on the winding breeze,
A story told amongst the trees.

With every footfall, magic is spun,
In the silence, where the wild things run.
A touch of frost on the wandering mind,
In the reverie, true peace we find.

Stars twinkle bright in the velvet night,
Crafting a canvas of pure delight.
As dreams entwine with the silvered air,
The heart awakens to moments rare.

A frosty kiss on the cheek of time,
Brings whispers of joy in rhythm and rhyme.
In this glistening world, thoughts take flight,
A frost-kissed reverie in the night.

The Winter's Soliloquy

In quiet chill the shadows creep,
Crystals glint where silence sleeps.
Beneath the sky, so vast and gray,
Whispers of frost begin to play.

A breath of frost, a gentle sigh,
Time drifts slow as clouds float by.
Each flake tells tales of days gone past,
Nature's slumber draped in white cast.

The world is hushed, wrapped in stillness,
Bitter winds bring a certain illness.
Yet in this cold, there's warmth inside,
Where memories of summer reside.

Fires crackle and shadows dance,
In cozy nooks, we dream and prance.
Hot cocoa sipped in tender pause,
Winter's grip holds us in its jaws.

As daylight fades, stars gleam bright,
A tapestry of hope in night.
In this solitude, I find my peace,
As winter's song will never cease.

Wandering Through Frozen Dreams

Through snow-laden paths, I wander free,
Where icy whispers call to me.
Veiled in white, the world anew,
A frozen dreamscape wrapped in hue.

Frosted trees stand tall and proud,
Their branches wear a crystal shroud.
In this silence, echoes play,
Marking moments of yesterday.

A meadow dressed in silver sheen,
Underneath, a hidden green.
The crunch of snow beneath my feet,
Nature's rhythm, oh so sweet.

Midst stillness, I hear the call,
Of winter's gift, its gentle thrall.
In this realm, I lose my way,
Yet find myself in soft decay.

Hearts entwined in candle glow,
Amidst the brume and falling snow.
Wandering dreams, a heart's embrace,
In frozen lands, I find my place.

The Solstice of Solitude

When daylight wanes and shadows loom,
The longest night carries its gloom.
Yet in the dark, stars come alive,
A celestial dance where dreams thrive.

Solitude wraps like winter's cloak,
A silent pact that we invoke.
In stillness, deep thoughts take flight,
Through crisp air, we find our light.

Nature holds her breath in time,
The world sways in gentle rhyme.
Whispers travel through the trees,
Carried softly on the breeze.

Icicles hang like crystal tears,
A reflection of lingering fears.
Yet in this hush, I find my strength,
Solstice shadows deliver length.

Firelight flickers, stories unfold,
In this embrace, I feel the bold.
As winter deepens, hope remains,
In solitude, my spirit gains.

Frosty Pathways

Beneath the boughs of frosted trees,
Whispers dance on the winter breeze.
Paths of white invite my tread,
Each step a story, softly said.

Misty mornings, a quiet grace,
Nature's tapestry, a delicate lace.
Footprints fade with the rising sun,
Marking where my thoughts have run.

Branches bend with a heavy load,
Guarding secrets on this road.
The hum of cold, a familiar song,
In this wilderness, where I belong.

Winter gems, the world aglow,
Touching magic in the snow.
Each frosty pathway I explore,
An invitation to seek more.

As twilight falls with a gentle sigh,
Colors merge in the evening sky.
In the hush of night, peace abounds,
Where frosty pathways weave their sounds.

An Antarctic Veil of Isolation

Snowflakes dance on icy air,
Whispers lost in frigid light.
Mountains loom, a silent stare,
Time stands still in endless white.

Loneliness drapes the frozen land,
Footsteps vanish, trails obscure.
Each breath echoes, a quiet hand,
Wrapping souls in crystal cure.

Shadows lengthen in the chill,
A horizon kissed by dusk.
Frost encircles, serene and still,
Guarding secrets, hushed and husk.

Silent waters, deep and vast,
Reflect the stars that coldly gleam.
In this realm, memories cast,
A fleeting, icy, whispered dream.

Amidst the vast and endless white,
Isolation finds its grace.
In frozen beauty, stark and bright,
Hearts entwine in this still place.

The Shimmering Sorrow of Winter's Embrace

Beneath a blanket soft and pale,
The world lies still, a frozen sigh.
Each flake a tale, a wistful trail,
Memories drift in the chilly sky.

In evening's glow, the shadows creep,
Branches bow under heaven's weight.
The silence deepens, secrets keep,
As night descends, the heart awaits.

Footsteps crunch on paths of frost,
Guided by the moon's soft glare.
In whispers cold, the warmth is lost,
Love lingers, yet feels so rare.

A shiver runs through winter's breath,
Echoes of laughter fade away.
In beauty lies the hint of death,
Where joy and sorrow blend and sway.

As snowflakes fall, a soft lament,
Weaving through the trees they roam.
Each glistening tear, a heart's descent,
Winter's grasp, forever home.

Emptiness Wrapped in White

Fields stretch endless, stark and bare,
A canvas bright, yet void of song.
The silence wrapped in frigid air,
Where shadows dwell, and echoes long.

Clouds hang low, a shroud of grey,
They whisper tales of dreams once sought.
In winter's grasp, they softly sway,
The warmth of life seems dearly bought.

Footsteps fade on powdery ground,
A journey lost in time's cruel clutch.
In emptiness, no solace found,
A fleeting touch, a gentle hush.

Glistening crystals catch the light,
Reflecting worlds we cannot reach.
Each breath condenses, pure and white,
A moment's pause, a silent speech.

A stillness falls, a hollow sound,
Within the snow, a heart laid bare.
In this emptiness, we are bound,
Wrapped in the cold, the weight we bear.

Frost-laden Winds and Aloof Thoughts

Through bitter winds, the whispers glide,
Each breath a ghost in twilight's glow.
Thoughts drift softly, lost in pride,
Carried on currents of silent snow.

The trees stand tall, adorned in ice,
Boughs bending with the weight of night.
In their stillness, there lies a price,
For beauty finds its strength in fright.

A chill wraps round the wandering mind,
Where solitude blooms in frozen air.
Memories swirl, unkindly entwined,
In the frost, a poignant despair.

With each gust, the heartbeats slow,
A dance with shadows, pale and dim.
Across the vast, white fields we go,
Searching for warmth, on a whim.

Yet in this cold, we find a spark,
A flicker of hope, a secret light.
Amidst the frost's relentless dark,
Our thoughts take flight, into the night.

The Silence of Snowdrifts

The snowflakes fall, so soft and light,
A blanket wraps the world in white,
Whispers of winter, calm and still,
Each flake a promise, each drift a will.

Silent woods where shadows play,
Nature's hush at the end of day,
Footprints fade in the gentle glow,
The beauty found in the silent snow.

Crisp air bites with a tender chill,
Time slows down, the heart can still,
In this moment, all worries cease,
Wrapped in nature's quilt of peace.

Icicles hang like glass-made spears,
They capture light and all our fears,
Yet here in this serene, white drape,
A canvas pure, the world takes shape.

Embrace the stillness, let it in,
In snowdrifts deep, we find our kin,
Each silence speaks, each flake does call,
In the winter's clutch, we can stand tall.

Tundra of the Soul

Endless expanse of white and gray,
A tundra stretches, come what may,
Barren beauty, harsh and true,
In solitude, the heart breaks through.

Whispers echo in frozen air,
Dreams wander without a care,
Unseen paths in the frosty haze,
Lost in the depth of winter's gaze.

Bold willows sway in a silent dance,
Their shadows flicker, a fleeting glance,
Life finds a way in this stark domain,
Resilience blooms despite the pain.

Footfalls muffled on ancient ground,
A serenity where peace is found,
In the vastness, the soul takes flight,
Finding warmth in the winter's night.

Nature's canvas, a quiet call,
In the tundra's arms, we find it all,
Each breath a bond to this land we hold,
A story whispered in silence bold.

Glacial Horizons

Rising peaks in a sapphire sky,
Glaciers gleam where the cold winds sigh,
Icebergs drift in an endless dance,
Under the spell of winter's trance.

The horizon stretches, vast and wide,
Frozen waves where secrets hide,
The heart whispers to the frosty air,
In this glacial grace, we lay bare.

Reflections shimmer on icy streams,
Caught in the web of our waking dreams,
A cool embrace in the fading light,
While stars awaken, igniting the night.

Nature's sculptures, a timeless art,
Each crevice shows a frozen heart,
Beneath the layers of frost and snow,
Lies the passage where histories flow.

In solitude, we carve our way,
Amidst glacial horizons, come what may,
For within this beauty, fierce and bold,
Lies a story of life, waiting to unfold.

Muffled Footsteps in Snow

Muffled footsteps mark the way,
In a world wrapped soft in gray,
Each step whispers a tale untold,
Of moments cherished, of warmth to hold.

The ground beneath, a quilted host,
With secrets buried, a silent boast,
Nature listens, and we confide,
In every crunch, our dreams reside.

Frosted branches, a gentle sway,
Framing paths where wild hearts play,
A journey lost in the snowy veil,
In this stillness, we set sail.

Echoes fade, but memories stay,
Muffled footsteps lead the way,
In winter's embrace, we find our place,
In the softness, we carve our space.

Gentle whispers, the night draws near,
As stars emerge, the sky sincere,
With each heartbeat, the world feels right,
In muffled footsteps, we're home tonight.

Dreaming in a Frosted Abyss

In the depths where silence sleeps,
Dreams arise from icy deeps.
Whispers of a forgotten time,
Entwined in a frozen rhyme.

Ghostly figures dance and sway,
Guiding lost souls on their way.
Through shadows cast by pale moon light,
They glide on wings of fragile night.

Each breath forms a crystal veil,
Stories linger in the pale.
Echoes of laughter softly blend,
In a realm where dreams ascend.

A tapestry of frost and dreams,
Weaving through the silver seams.
In the abyss, all is still,
A haunting echo of the chill.

Here in stillness, hope ignites,
In the heart of winter nights.
Amongst the frost, we find our way,
Dreaming deep till break of day.

Shadows Drifting in Subzero Stillness

Beneath the stars, shadows creep,
In the cold where echoes weep.
Each motion cloaked in frigid air,
Whispers cling to the moonlight's glare.

Frozen branches sway and bend,
As the night begins to send.
Messages through the icy breeze,
Carried softly, meant to please.

In this stillness, time is lost,
The heart feels numb to the cost.
Yet in the quiet, truth reveals,
A warmth that only silence heals.

Drifting through the midnight blue,
Each heartbeat steady, calm, and true.
Shadows dance like fading dreams,
Capturing the light in streams.

In subzero beckons' hold,
Stories whispered, brave and bold.
Together forged, we will remain,
In the frost, where love holds reign.

The Crystal Chorus of Solitary Nights

In solitary night's embrace,
A crystal chorus finds its place.
Notes of winter, sharp and clear,
Resonate in the quiet sphere.

Each glimmer catches fading light,
Creating melodies of ice so bright.
Harmony within the cold,
A symphony of stories told.

The stillness hums a gentle song,
In the darkness, we belong.
Frosty whispers fill the air,
Reminders that the heart can care.

Echoes drift on winds that chill,
Binding souls with winter's will.
Together weaves a subtle thread,
Of dreams awakened, lightly spread.

Beneath the vast, star-lit sky,
The crystal chorus echoes high.
A serenade of longing and grace,
In solitary night's warm embrace.

Whispering Pines in the Depths of Cold

Whispering pines in the frosty night,
Guard secrets held out of sight.
Softly swaying, they stand tall,
Silent watchers of nature's call.

In the depths where shadows loom,
They cradle the earth, ward off gloom.
Their sighs mix with the winter air,
Bringing solace, always there.

Underneath their blanket wide,
A refuge where the lost can hide.
Branches cradling the dreams we weave,
In the cold, they gently believe.

As the stars blink in the sky,
Pines whisper tales, low and shy.
Through the hush, their voices flow,
A serenade of winter's glow.

In their embrace, the world stands still,
Nature's heart beats with a thrill.
Whispering pines, ever bold,
In the depths, their wonders unfold.

A Heart Encased in Winter's Grasp

In silence deep, the cold winds blow,
A heart confined where shadows grow.
Whispers of love lost in the frost,
Memories linger, but warmth is tossed.

Frosted branches, a trembling sigh,
Beneath the chill, old hopes lie dry.
Time weaves blankets of icy despair,
Yet still, the embers flicker somewhere.

Through barren trees, the moonlight glows,
Illuminates the pain that flows.
A fragile beat, this frozen heart,
Hopes thaw with spring, a brand new start.

Wrapped in layers of white and gray,
The longing cries for brighter days.
Yet here in silence, beauty's found,
In winter's hold, a love profound.

So let the snow fall crisp and pure,
For even ice can feel love's lure.
A heart encased may yet ignite,
In winter's grasp, a flame burns bright.

The Solace of Crystal Stillness

In crystal stillness, time stands still,
A breath held tight, a moment's thrill.
Each flake that falls, a dream takes flight,
Embracing peace within the night.

The world adorned in icy lace,
Nature whispers, a gentle grace.
Through quiet woods, the stillness hums,
A melody where silence comes.

Beneath the stars, the landscape glows,
Reflecting calm where serenity flows.
Each heartbeat pulses, slow and deep,
In this embrace, my soul shall keep.

As dawn awakens in shades of gold,
The warmth of sun, a story told.
Yet in the hush of frosted air,
I find my heart without a care.

The solace found in winter's hold,
In every flake, a tale retold.
With every breath, my spirit flies,
In crystal stillness, my heart lies.

Luminous Solitudes Beneath the Glare of Ice

Beneath the glare of ice so bright,
Lies solitude wrapped in quiet light.
A world transformed in shimmering white,
Where shadows dance with the pale moonlight.

Each breath exhales a frosty sigh,
As time turns slow and the moments lie.
In solitude's bloom, I find my peace,
Where nature's sigh brings a sweet release.

The chill caresses with tender grace,
In this embrace, my heart finds place.
Glances exchanged with the stars above,
In timeless solitude, I feel love.

Across the tundra, whispers flow,
In sparkling silence, the wonders grow.
Beneath the ice, a world unseen,
In luminous dreams where I have been.

As dawn breaks soft with hues anew,
The solitude sings of a love so true.
In every flake, a story's spun,
Beneath the glare, we are but one.

The Permafrost of Unspoken Thoughts

In permafrost where feelings freeze,
Unspoken words hang in the breeze.
Like frozen rivers, they run deep,
In shadows dark, my secrets keep.

Each breath a puff of smoky air,
In this still world, I lay my care.
Thoughts crystallize beneath the weight,
Of icy dreams that hesitate.

A heart entangled, soft yet strong,
Yearns for the light, where it belongs.
But here in silence, hope does tread,
In frozen blooms, my heart is spread.

Time drips slowly, an hourglass,
With grains of hope, like summer grass.
Yet deep within this frozen shell,
A fire dances, dreams to tell.

So let the thaw come, gently grace,
Unveiling fears I must embrace.
In permafrost, I'll find my way,
To break the ice and greet the day.

Glacial Reflections in a Quiet Mind

In a still lake mirrors lie,
Thoughts like whispers, soft and shy.
Chilled air wraps around the trees,
Silent moments, carried breeze.

Frosted edges lace the ground,
Peaceful echoes, barely a sound.
Nature's artwork, pure and bright,
Shards of crystal, morning light.

Gentle ripples break the calm,
Mind at ease with nature's balm.
Each reflection speaks a truth,
Frozen memories of youth.

Clouds drift slowly, painted gray,
In this quiet, thoughts can play.
Serenity in every glance,
Glacial movements in a dance.

Moments linger, rich and rare,
Every breath a whispered prayer.
In the stillness, life unfolds,
Glacial secrets to be told.

The Desolate Beauty of Frozen Tranquility

White blankets cover silent lands,
No footprints mark the untouched sands.
A fragile peace in icy hues,
Nature's stillness, vast and blue.

Underneath the silvered skies,
Frosty whispers, nature sighs.
Each branch heavy with crystal light,
A desolate beauty, pure delight.

Lonely valleys stretch ahead,
Where once vibrant life had tread.
Now only echoes fill the air,
In frozen spaces, thoughts laid bare.

A tranquil world, eerily calm,
Holding memories like a psalm.
In the stillness, time stands still,
The beauty of it, a frigid thrill.

Frozen lakes mirror the dawn,
A world reborn, yet almost gone.
Desolation dressed in white,
Beauty found in quiet night.

Chilling Solitudes Beneath the Stars

Beneath the sky, cold worlds collide,
Chilling whispers, secrets hide.
Stars like diamonds, distant calls,
In the vastness, silence falls.

Lonely spirits roam the night,
Finding solace in starlight bright.
Frozen breath, a fleeting mist,
In this stillness, dreams persist.

Night unfurls her velvet cloak,
Among the pines, shadows joke.
Echoing sounds of soft despair,
Chilling solitudes fill the air.

Every twinkle tells a tale,
Of frozen lands where dreams set sail.
In solitude, the heart can soar,
Amidst the chill, we seek for more.

Wandering thoughts dance in the night,
In starry realms, we find our light.
Chilling moments, deep and vast,
Beneath the stars, we hold them fast.

Frostbitten Memories of Forgotten Days

Beneath the frost, old tales await,
Memories woven, delicate fate.
In the whispers of azure skies,
Echoes linger, soft goodbyes.

Broken branches hold their weight,
Frostbitten dreams anticipate.
Each flake a memory in flight,
Forgotten days wrapped in white.

Steam rises with the morning sun,
Ghosts of laughter, lost in fun.
In the stillness, stories roam,
Frostbitten hearts find their home.

Glimpses of laughter, shadows long,
Time's embrace, a gentle song.
In the cold, we chart our way,
Frostbitten memories shall stay.

Every chill brings us back to grace,
Winter wears a sacred face.
Fading echoes of brighter days,
In frost's embrace, the soul displays.

Shivering in Stillness

The frost clings tight to every breath,
As shadows stretch beneath the trees.
A whisper dances, pondering death,
In this frozen world, it's hard to freeze.

Each flake a secret, carefully spun,
Whirling softly in the pale moonlight.
In stillness, fading, one by one,
They kiss the ground, a ghostly sight.

The winds do speak, though soft and low,
Telling tales of the winter's grace.
Beneath the stars, the cold will grow,
Yet life persists in this quiet place.

With every heartbeat, silence reigns,
A world adorned in icy lace.
Through shivering veins, the winter pains,
But still we stand, unyielding face.

Embraced by shadows, lost in thought,
We ponder all that winter brings.
In every corner, battles fought,
Life finds a way despite the sting.

The Chilling Pull of Silence

In the quiet hush of evening's fall,
A blanket soft, the world holds tight.
Whispers linger, faint and small,
As stars awaken, hearts take flight.

The air is thick with heavy dreams,
A longing echo, raw and deep.
In every shadow, the silence seems
To cradle sorrows, press and keep.

Here, time stands still, it softly weaves,
A web of thoughts, both dark and light.
In solitude, the spirit grieves,
Yet finds a spark, a flicker bright.

The chilling pull draws us near,
With every breath, a gentle sway.
We listen close, to what we fear,
Yet hope persists, not far away.

As night descends, the heart finds peace,
In silence, burdens fall away.
With every moment, fears release,
And let the dawn bring forth the day.

Solitary Flurries

A flurry falls, serenely shy,
With each small patch of white so pure.
It spirals down from winter's sky,
In this moment, hearts endure.

The world is hushed, a fragile thing,
As solitude wraps every sound.
In quiet corners, angels sing,
In solitude, lost dreams are found.

Beneath the weight of all that's gone,
A whisper stirs in the chilly air.
These solitary flurries carry on,
With stories wrapped in silver flare.

Each flake a thought, a fleeting sigh,
In the fleeting dance of time's retreat.
As warmth prepares to bid goodbye,
These moments linger, bittersweet.

So let us treasure every twirl,
In winter's grasp, we find our way.
As flurries spin and gently swirl,
They mark the end, they greet the day.

Midwinter Reverie

In dreams of frost, the night unfolds,
A canvas blank, untouched by light.
Each breath a story, softly told,
As shadows stretch, embracing night.

The stars hold secrets in their glow,
While whispers dance upon the breeze.
In midwinter's grip, our hearts will know,
A tender peace, a soul at ease.

Each flake that falls, a note in song,
Weaving magic as they play.
In this stillness, we belong,
Bound by dreams that drift away.

With every twilight, warmth arrives,
A glimmer in the chilly air.
In reverie, our spirit thrives,
A fleeting touch, a gentle care.

And as the dawn begins to break,
We cherish all that winter gave.
In every heartbeat, love will wake,
A melody, forever brave.

The Frosty Cloak of Being Alone

In the stillness of the night,
Whispers echo through the trees,
A heart wrapped in silent frost,
Yearning for warmth, yet at ease.

Footsteps crunch on the icy ground,
Each one a lonely song unfurls,
Stars hang low, like distant dreams,
In shadows dance the frozen swirls.

The air bites with a bitter chill,
Yet solace finds a place to dwell,
In solitude's embrace lies peace,
A frosty cloak, a quiet shell.

Branches bare and skies so grey,
The world feels heavy, yet it sighs,
For in this silence, strength is forged,
A truth that never wears a disguise.

Loneliness, a fleeting guest,
Brings with it the quiet grace,
In every flake that tumbles down,
Life's fragile beauty finds its place.

Solace in Subdued Glimmers of Light

Drifting clouds in twilight's hold,
Softly weave the dusk to night,
Stars awaken, delicate gems,
Filling darkness with gentle light.

Through branches sway the winter's breath,
A chill that sparkles with soft dreams,
Each twinkle holds a whisper's grace,
Beneath their glow, the silence beams.

In cracked paths of unyielding frost,
Hope arises with each tender glance,
For amidst the chilly, muted hues,
There lies a chance for soft romance.

Night enfolds the weary heart,
Yet flickers guide through veils of gloom,
In subdued glimmers, strength will find,
A way to flourish, even bloom.

With every breath, the world transforms,
Where shadows dance with fleeting flame,
In solace, seek the warmth of stars,
And find peace within the name.

A Canvas of White and Silent Reflections

Winter paints with purest white,
A canvas stretched beneath the skies,
Each flake a whisper from above,
In silence, beauty softly lies.

Footprints trail through the powdery snow,
Every step a tale concealed,
In stark contrast, colors blended,
Nature's artwork, gently revealed.

Mirrors glimmer from icy streams,
Reflecting dreams of days gone past,
The world, a masterpiece in time,
In tranquil whispers, shadows cast.

Boughs laden with a silver sheen,
Hold secrets in their frozen grip,
As silence swirls in delicate arcs,
And memories begin to slip.

Yet in this stillness, hearts can mend,
For in reflections, truth does shine,
A canvas wide with hope reborn,
The art of winter, pure and divine.

Winter's Grasp on a Fragile Heart

Beneath the weight of winter's chill,
A heart beats soft with gentle sighs,
In layers thick, it seeks to hide,
From all the cold, the biting lies.

Yet through the frost, a spark escapes,
A warmth that flickers, faint but bright,
In every shadow of despair,
Resilience weaves its threads of light.

The world outside is cold and stark,
But deep within, a fire glows,
In fragile beats of whispered love,
Life's tenderness in silence grows.

Winter's grasp may feel so strong,
But hearts, like flowers, crave the sun,
With each new dawn, the frost will break,
And fragile hopes will see them run.

So hold your heart against the cold,
For spring shall come with brighter days,
In every breath, a promise speaks,
That warmth will chase the frost away.

Solitude's Hush Beneath the Snow

In the stillness of the night,
Whispers drift, soft and slow.
Blanketed dreams take flight,
Solitude's hush beneath the snow.

Cold stars flicker in the gaze,
Of a moon that shimmers bright.
Nature's breath, a gentle phrase,
In the calm of winter's night.

Footprints vanish, lost and gone,
Leaving secrets soft and low.
Each moment drawn like dusk at dawn,
Solitude's hush beneath the snow.

Trees stand tall in silence deep,
Guardians of this frozen show.
They hold the whispers, secrets keep,
In the stillness, hearts aglow.

As the world sleeps, time drifts by,
In a blanket thin and flow.
Among the dreams, I softly sigh,
Solitude's hush beneath the snow.

Heartbeats Lost in Winter's Breath

Beneath the frost, the silence beats,
Echoes of whispers from afar.
Where heartbeats dance with icy feet,
Lost in the glow of the night star.

Branches sway in the chilling air,
Shadows play on the ground below.
Memories linger, rich and rare,
Heartbeats lost in winter's breath, so slow.

Steps left imprints on the snow,
Stories etched in emerald green.
A fleeting warmth begins to show,
As heartbeats pulse, though unseen.

Crystals twinkle on blankets white,
Nature's shimmer, a soft show.
Each frozen breath ignites the night,
Heartbeats lost in winter's breath, aglow.

In this refuge, peace unfolds,
As time drifts on, a gentle flow.
In winter's grasp, a tale retold,
Heartbeats lost in winter's breath.

A Lonesome Shelter of Frozen Walls

In a realm where silence reigns,
Frozen walls, stark and tall.
Whispers echo through the plains,
A lonesome shelter of frozen walls.

Snowflakes swirl in dances bright,
Tracing patterns, soft and small.
In the hush, they twirl with light,
A lonesome shelter of frozen walls.

The chill wraps close, an icy shroud,
Pressing secrets where shadows crawl.
Bound in quiet, fierce and proud,
A lonesome shelter of frozen walls.

Time stands still in winter's grasp,
Moments drift like a soft ball.
Hold your breath, and let it clasp,
A lonesome shelter of frozen walls.

With each heartbeat, life shall grow,
Hope ignites amidst the thrall.
Through the frost, we come to know,
A lonesome shelter of frozen walls.

Respite Beneath the Arctic Sky

Underneath the endless blue,
A world wrapped in crystal light.
In the quiet, hearts renew,
Respite beneath the Arctic sky.

Whispers of cold drift so near,
Echoes of dreams begin to fly.
In solitude, we lose our fear,
Respite beneath the Arctic sky.

Gentle winds weave songs of peace,
Nature's lullaby draws nigh.
In this moment, worries cease,
Respite beneath the Arctic sky.

The dawn breaks with a soft embrace,
Painting colors, warm and shy.
In every breath, find solace,
Respite beneath the Arctic sky.

Finding warmth in frozen realms,
Where hearts beat strong, and spirits sigh.
In this haven, we are the helms,
Respite beneath the Arctic sky.

The Echoes of Solitary Footprints

Beneath the pale moonlight's gaze,
Footprints whisper ancient ways.
Through the hush of midnight's call,
Lonely echoes gently fall.

Softly tracing each step made,
In a world that seems to fade.
Stories linger in the night,
Silent pathways, lost in flight.

Every step, a tale unfolds,
Of secrets whispered, dreams retold.
Nature cradles all that's near,
In the stillness, all is clear.

With each print upon the ground,
Footsteps fade without a sound.
Yet in shadows, life persists,
In the void, hope still exists.

As dawn arrives with tender light,
The footprints vanish out of sight.
Yet in the hearts that still roam,
The echoes find a place called home.

Lonesome Stars in a Frozen Sky

In the chill of midnight blue,
Lonesome stars, a frosty view.
Whispers travel through the void,
In their glow, the night enjoyed.

Each twinkle tells of silent dreams,
Lost in time, or so it seems.
Beneath the vast and icy dome,
Wandering hearts find no true home.

Galaxies dance in spectral light,
Navigating through the night.
Hopeful wishes cast afar,
Chasing down a distant star.

Yet amidst the frozen air,
The lonesome sighs admit a prayer.
May the warmth of love be near,
In the cold, a voice to hear.

In silence, dreams ignite the sky,
As lonesome stars watch and sigh.
Though alone, they shine so bright,
Guiding souls through endless night.

Chasing Shadows in a Winter's Dream

Beneath the blanket, soft and white,
Shadows dance in silver light.
In the hush of winter's breath,
The world embraces quiet death.

Footsteps linger, softly tread,
Chasing whispers of the dead.
Every flake that tumbles down,
Hides secrets lost in icy town.

Dreams entwined in frosty air,
The quiet heart learns how to dare.
Through the frosts of time's disdain,
Memories drift like falling rain.

In a world where silence reigns,
Chasing shadows eases pains.
Winter's grip, a gentle chain,
Binding souls that bear the strain.

Yet within this dreamy light,
Hope arises, faint but bright.
Through the shadows, pathways gleam,
Leading hearts towards the dream.

Solitary Glances through Frosted Windows

Through frosted panes, the world grows dim,
Solitary glances, cold and grim.
In stillness wrapped by winter's hand,
Loneliness within us stands.

Each breath fogs the glass with doubt,
Inside the warmth, we dream about.
Life unfolds in muted hues,
A scene alive, yet cold to choose.

Fingers trace the icy streaks,
Searching solace, silence speaks.
Outside the world seems far away,
In the stillness, hearts will sway.

Yet eyes hold stories yet untold,
In each glance, a life unfolds.
Through each frost, a soft embrace,
Solitude, a sacred space.

Though windows shield from winter's bite,
They cannot dim the inner light.
In solitude, we come to see,
The beauty in our quiet plea.

Milton Keynes UK
Ingram Content Group UK Ltd.
UKHW010232111224
452348UK00011B/702